EFFECTIVE VIDEOCONFERENCING
Techniques for Better Business Meetings

Lynn Diamond, Ph.D.
Stephanie Roberts

A FIFTY-MINUTE™ SERIES BOOK

CRISP PUBLICATIONS, INC.
Menlo Park, California

EFFECTIVE VIDEOCONFERENCING
Techniques for Better Business Meetings

Lynn Diamond, Ph.D.
Stephanie Roberts

CREDITS
Managing Editor: **Kathleen Barcos**
Editor: **Kay Keppler**
Typesetting: **ExecuStaff**
Artwork: **Ralph Mapson**
Cover Design: **Carol Harris**

Copyright © 1996 by Crisp Publications, Inc.

Printed in the United States of America by Bawden Printing Company.

English language Crisp books are distributed worldwide. Our major international distributors include:

CANADA: Reid Publishing Ltd., Box 69559–109 Thomas St., Oakville, Ontario, Canada L6J 7R4. TEL: (905) 842-4428, FAX: (905) 842-9327

Raincoast Books Distribution Ltd., 112 East 3rd Avenue, Vancouver, British Columbia, Canada V5T 1C8. TEL: (604) 873-6581, FAX: (604) 874-2711

AUSTRALIA: Career Builders, P.O. Box 1051, Springwood, Brisbane, Queensland, Australia 4127. TEL: 841-1061, FAX: 841-1580

NEW ZEALAND: Career Builders, P.O. Box 571, Manurewa, Auckland, New Zealand. TEL: 266-5276, FAX: 266-4152

JAPAN: Phoenix Associates Co., Mizuho Bldg. 2-12-2, Kami Osaki, Shinagawa-Ku, Tokyo 141, Japan. TEL: 3-443-7231, FAX: 3-443-7640

Selected Crisp titles are also available in other languages. Contact International Rights Manager Suzanne Kelly at (415) 323-6100 for more information.

Library of Congress Catalog Card Number 95-68747
Diamond, Lynn and Stephanie Roberts
Effective Videoconferencing
ISBN 1-56052-354-9

This book is printed on recyclable paper with soy ink.

ABOUT THIS BOOK

Effective Videoconferencing is an easy-to-use guide to videoconferencing for anyone who works collaboratively with others at a distance. Its objective is to enable you to combine effective meeting techniques with state-of-the-art videoconferencing technology for productive, interactive meetings in the age of global communications.

NOTE: *Effective Videoconferencing* focuses on how to plan and conduct two-way videoconference meetings. Selecting and installing a videoconferencing system is beyond the scope of this book, as is the specialized use of videoconferencing for one-way satellite broadcasts (business television).

Effective Videoconferencing can be used effectively in a number of ways. Here are some possibilities:

Individual Study. Because the book is self-instructional, all that is needed is a quiet place, some time and a pencil. Completing the activities and exercises should provide not only valuable feedback, but also practical ideas for identifying and developing videoconferencing possibilities.

Workshops and Seminars. This book is ideal for preassigned reading prior to a workshop or seminar. With the basics in hand, the quality of participation should improve. More time can be spent on concept extensions and applications during the program. The book is also effective when distributed at the beginning of a session.

Remote Location Training. Copies can be sent to those not able to attend "home office" training sessions.

Informal Study Groups. Thanks to the format, brevity and low cost, this book is ideal for "brown-bag" or other informal group sessions.

There are other possibilities that depend on the objectives of the user. One thing is certain: even after it has been read, this book will serve as excellent reference material that can be easily reviewed. Good luck!

ABOUT THE AUTHORS

Lynn Diamond, Ph.D., is president of Innovative Information Techniques, Inc., a training and communications consulting firm in New York City. In addition to giving keynote addresses and conducting productivity enhancing seminars, Lynn provides one-to-one executive development coaching for Fortune 500 executives. She has been an officer of the American Society for Training and Development and is a member of the National Speakers Association.

Stephanie Roberts is an instructional designer and technical writer whose programs on such topics as innovation, leadership, and adapting to change have helped corporate clients improve performance and productivity. She has written leaders' guides, video scripts, reference books and other educational materials.

ACKNOWLEDGMENTS

Thanks are due to Virginia Ostendorf for enhancing our advice on videoconferencing presentation skills. Glenn Kaufman of the New York Videoconference Center very generously shared his time, technical knowledge, and experiences with us. Permission to incorporate their expertise is gratefully acknowledged.

The method for tracking interaction presented in "Section Six: Leading the Meeting; Managing Participation," is adapted from copyright material developed by Virginia A. Ostendorf in *The Two-Way Video Classroom* (Picture Telearning Edition). Used by permission of the author.

CONTENTS

CONTENTS (continued)

TO THE READER

We live and work in a truly global age. Often, we need to collaborate with people in other organizations, cities and countries—and we don't have the time or the budget to travel. Videoconferencing is a unique solution to the communication and information-sharing needs of today's organizations.

Videoconferencing permits you to use resources more efficiently and manage your projects more effectively. It is a powerful tool for competitive advantage in the global information age, and it is transforming how we work with and learn from each other both within and between organizations.

Industry analysts predict that by the end of the decade, videoconferencing equipment will be as fundamental a part of our working environment as the personal computer and the fax machine are today. And it promises to be just as revolutionary to the way we do business as the personal computer and the fax machine have been. If you haven't used videoconferencing yet, you will soon!

Successful videoconferencing is a new kind of group communication. It requires new skills and new ways of doing things, and that's what this book is about. It is a workbook in the true sense of the word, guiding you step-by-step through every stage of planning and conducting a successful videoconference.

So get out your pencil and roll up your sleeves—we're about to take the mystery out of videoconferencing and show you just how easy and exciting it can be!

Lynn Diamond   Stephanie Roberts

SECTION

I

What Videoconferencing Can Do for You

WHAT IS VIDEOCONFERENCING?

Videoconferencing adds video images to voice telecommunication among two or more locations. It creates a "virtual reality" of being in the same room with people who may be thousands of miles away. You can do virtually anything in a video-conference that you would do in an in-person meeting—hold discussions, create and display graphics, demonstrate products and more.

You may be using a dedicated videoconferencing room with built-in equipment, a portable system, "rollabout" set up in a conference room or a rent-by-the-hour public room. The trend is toward desktop systems integrated with a personal computer. Desktop videoconferencing offers all the benefits of a traditional system, plus shared-document collaborative computing.

Whatever type of system you use, videoconferencing is an easy and effective way to work with others at a distance. It will expand your office to encompass the world.

WHEN IS VIDEOCONFERENCING APPROPRIATE?

Many people use videoconferencing only when they want to avoid the cost and inconvenience of travel. In many other situations, however, videoconferencing is a better choice than communicating by telephone, E-Mail or fax.

Because it enables interactive discussions and graphic illustration, videoconferencing is the perfect medium for issues that may raise questions or require clarification. When people from different departments or organizations are involved in joint projects, it can help create a stronger feeling of teamwork.

Use this table to help you decide when to use videoconferencing (VC) and when to use the phone, E-Mail or fax.

COMMUNICATION ISSUES	VC	Phone	E-Mail	Fax
Communication is one-way			✔	✔
Communication is two-way	✔	✔		
Information is time-sensitive	✔	✔	✔	✔
Information needs to go to several locations at once	✔	✔	✔	✔
Immediate feedback/interaction is desired	✔	✔		
Input from several locations is desired	✔			
Visual clarification may be required	✔			
People from different departments/organizations are involved	✔			
Discussion items will include objects, graphics, or computer files	✔			
The people involved have not met before	✔			

APPLICATIONS AND BENEFITS

The most widely recognized benefits of videoconferencing are the time and cost savings that result when people in different places no longer have to travel in order to meet together. The strategic advantages of videoconferencing, however, go far beyond travel-related dollars. To many organizations, time and productivity benefits are of greater long-term importance than the money saved from reduced travel.

Six strategic advantages to be gained through videoconferencing are described on the following pages, with examples of applications that have been used to achieve those advantages.

The sample applications come from many industries, but the benefits can be achieved by anyone. Regardless of your industry, business or organization, videoconferencing can help you be more effective with less hassle. You might videoconference with a customer half-way around the world this morning and with a colleague on another floor of your building this afternoon.

As you read about how others have used videoconferencing, think about how you can apply the technology in your own job. Record your ideas in the space provided on the following pages.

APPLICATIONS AND BENEFITS (continued)

Strategic Advantage #1: More Productive Time in the Office

The typical overnight business trip costs more than travel, room and board; there's also the hidden cost of lost productive time. In spite of notebook computers and in-flight phones, the value of useful time lost during travel can still be more than twice the cost of the trip.

Add to this the wear and tear of traveling early in the morning or after a full day at the office, being away from home, jet lag, fatigue and the stress of too many trips to too many places in too short a time. Given the travel schedules of many of today's managers and executives, it's a wonder we are in any shape to work at all. Videoconferencing won't keep you off the road completely, but it will result in less time spent traveling and more productive time in your office.

Application

Fewer Short Trips

Videoconferencing is as useful on a local level as it is for connecting across great distances. One busy executive gains hours of productive time every month by videoconferencing with colleagues instead of making a frequent five-minute walk to another building just a few blocks away.

I can use videoconferencing to reduce travel time and costs for:

_____

_____

_____

Strategic Advantage #2: Strengthened Teamwork

Through videoconferencing, people in separate locations feel more like part of a team. Senior executives can make more frequent appearances to remote constituents, and people at all levels of the organization can contribute to meetings they otherwise might not attend.

Applications

Bringing Regional Offices into the Loop

A nationwide transportation provider now uses videoconferencing to include regional managers in daily staff meetings. Before, these managers met with headquarters staff only on a quarterly basis.

Regular videoconference meetings with the home office have helped satellite offices of a consumer products company feel more a part of the team. Corporate commitment to improved communication is demonstrated clearly and effectively, encouraging an open exchange of ideas and strengthening field-to-headquarters relationships.

Forging a Multinational Team

Multinational organizations communicating through videoconferencing can experience a sense of unity that strengthens the company as a whole. A leading automotive corporation enabled design teams in the United States, Germany and England to collaborate on a new car design through videoconferencing. They discovered that international work teams are more productive when language barriers are reduced because they see as well as talk with their global partners.

I can use videoconferencing to improve teamwork by:

_____

_____

_____

APPLICATIONS AND BENEFITS (continued)

> ## Strategic Advantage #3: Better Customer/ Supplier Relationships

Videoconferencing offers many opportunities for more productive relationships with your customers and suppliers.

Applications

Customer Service

Customers can be trained in how to use a product through videoconferenced instruction. Sales reps and technical support personnel meet with customers more effectively than by phone for improved responsiveness and faster troubleshooting.

Greater Customer Involvement

An advertising agency in Manhattan videoconferences regularly with a client in New Jersey to plan new product introductions. Because meetings are more frequent, the client has greater input, and new directions can be taken before the agency develops a costly presentation. Campaigns are more on-target throughout the development process, and the client is better pleased with the result.

Communication with Vendors

One telecommunications company conducts periodic videoconference reviews with key vendors. More people are included, everyone gets the same information at the same time, and vendors no longer need to make multiple presentations.

I can use videoconferencing to improve customer/supplier relationships by:

_____

_____

_____

Strategic Advantage #4: Faster, Better Decision Making

Videoconferencing can help you get the information you need from key experts or stakeholders, so you can make timely, better-informed decisions.

Applications

Joint Problem Solving

A manufacturer with multiple plant sites holds regular joint problem-solving meetings. Knowledgeable workers have input into the solutions, and weeks are shaved off the time spent solving problems that were once tackled by each plant individually.

Broader Information Base

Regional sales and marketing managers for an automotive products manufacturer meet easily and frequently to brainstorm ways to increase sales and target new markets. Since all relevant people take part, ideas are given first-hand and questions are addressed immediately. Decisions are made based on a broad range of input, not just on local factors.

Crisis Management

Through videoconferencing, crises can be addressed promptly with a minimum of upheaval. For example, a multilocation company used videoconferencing to respond rapidly to a computer virus. They were able to alert many locations simultaneously of the potential threat and to organize a sweep of all PCs.

I can use videoconferencing for faster, better decision-making in these areas/ projects:

_____

_____

_____

APPLICATIONS AND BENEFITS (continued)

Strategic Advantage #5: More Effective Project Management

Through videoconferencing, collaboration on multilocation projects becomes easier and ideas are shared more freely. The number of delays caused by poor communication can often be significantly reduced.

Applications

Technical Collaboration

Videoconferencing eliminates a lot of the confusion that results when technical details are discussed over the telephone, because everyone can see the part or drawing they're talking about. When engineering and production groups collaborated through videoconferencing, an aeronautics corporation cut 30 days from the development of its latest jet aircraft.

Facilities Management

An information technologies company was able to consolidate several large data centers into a single location by using videoconferencing to coordinate critical day-to-day activities from a central site.

More Productive Follow-Up Visits

On-site visits become more productive when they follow up on videoconferenced discussions. Because everyone has had a clearer, more direct understanding of the desired outcome, fewer issues need to be clarified or revised and more time is spent moving ahead.

I can use videoconferencing to manage these projects more effectively:

_____

_____

_____

Strategic Advantage #6: Competitive Edge

Videoconferencing is a tool for competitive success in virtually any area of your organization because it enables you to do more with fewer resources in less time.

Applications

Hiring the Best

Human resources executives at the New York headquarters of a global cosmetics industry giant regularly interview job candidates in Europe and the Far East via videoconferencing for fast, cost-effective staffing of key positions.

Speed to Market

A pharmaceutical company used videoconferencing with FDA representatives to clarify requirements for a new product application. The company beat its competition to the market and gained six months of patent exclusivity.

Developing Customer-Driven Products

A consumer products manufacturer conducts multiple focus groups at different locations all in the same day. More staff from cross-functional areas such as market research and product development can participate in the sessions.

Faster, Cost-Effective Training

A manufacturer trained a corporate-wide audience on a new order-fulfillment system, without expensive and time-consuming travel to individual sites for the trainers and with minimal time off the job for trainees.

I can use videoconferencing to achieve a competitive edge by:

_____

_____

SECRET TO SUCCESS

The more you use videoconferencing, the more applications you will think of. Come back to these pages from time to time to review, add to, and expand upon your ideas.

S E C T I O N

II

Learning About Your System

EXPECTATIONS AND REALITY

"If it looks like a TV, why doesn't it look like TV?"

Videoconferencing is not broadcast television. Three main differences are:

1. PICTURE

Most videoconferencing systems use two digital phone channels for transmission. A commercial television broadcast using the same equipment would require almost 1,400 phone lines, so some difference in picture quality is to be expected! Motion seen on a videoconference monitor is not as smooth as it is on television. The bigger the movement, the jerkier the picture is likely to be: more visual information has to be transmitted, and if the system backs up it will drop a few frames to stay in real time.

2. SOUND

The sound you hear during a videoconference will be the same as or a little better than your average telephone conversation. The biggest complaint most new users have is a slight delay in sound transmission, similar to that experienced in some intercontinental telephone calls. This delay occurs because sound data has to be coded and compressed for digital transmission, then decompressed and decoded on the other end. The delay is slight but noticeable and is easily handled by pausing to make sure the person at the other site has finished speaking before you begin.

3. INTERACTION

Television trains us to be passive, relaxed observers. We "watch" TV, but we are expected to "participate" in a videoconference. At first, it can seem strange to talk back to the monitor. As the meeting leader, it will be your responsibility to encourage interaction until everyone is participating comfortably.

TYPES OF VIDEOCONFERENCES

Videoconferencing systems have one or more of these capabilities. Check those that apply to the system you will use.

☐ **Multipoint-to-Multipoint**

Both audio and video transmissions are two-way among multiple sites, although you can hear and see only one other site at a time.

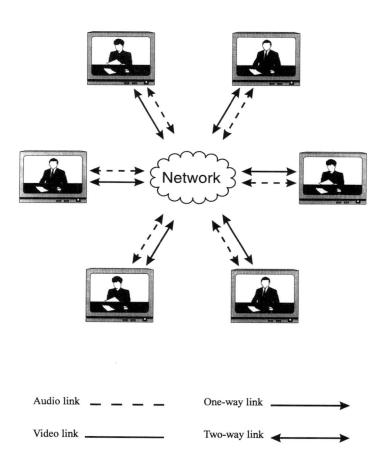

Audio link	- - - -	One-way link	⟶
Video link	————	Two-way link	⟷

☐ Point-to-Multipoint

Video is one-way: it originates at one site and is received at multiple sites. Audio is two-way: all sites can hear each other. Point-to-multipoint is frequently used for distance training.

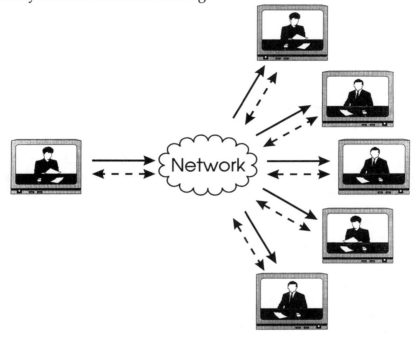

☐ Point-to-Point

Some systems can hook up with only one other site at a time. Video for this type of system may be one-way. However, if you use a system with multipoint capability for a two-site meeting, that conference also is called point-to-point and both audio and video will be two-way.

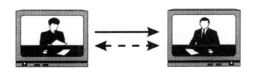

VIDEOCONFERENCING NETWORKS

Wide Area Networks

Traditional videoconferencing takes place over wide-area networks (WANs) provided by long-distance carriers such as AT&T, MCI and U.S. Sprint. If I'm on the Sprint WAN, but you're with AT&T, our conference may have to be scheduled several days in advance while my network makes arrangements to connect my system to your network and equipment.

Fortunately, *switched access digital networks* are becoming the norm. With switched access, you can connect to any WAN as easily as making a long-distance telephone call, regardless of carrier. The most widely used types of switched access are *switched 56* and *ISDN* (Integrated Services Digital Network).

Bandwidth, measured in bits per second, determines how much information can flow between sites. Wider bandwidths provide clearer pictures and smoother on-screen motion. Most WAN videoconferencing systems combine two 56K or 64K channels for 112K or 128K bandwidths.

Our carrier is: _____

My WAN network is:

☐ Switched 56   bandwidth: _____

☐ ISDN   bandwidth: _____

☐ Something else: _____

Desktop Networks (Computer-Based)

A desktop system may operate within a local area network (LAN) of linked computers within your department or organization and/or be connected to a WAN. For example, you might work on a spreadsheet with Chris in Marketing via the LAN within your Chicago office. Then, you and Chris might join a videoconference with Pat and Amy in Santa Fe, from your desks, via a WAN link. Collaborative computing—working on shared files with the other people in your videoconference—may not be possible during a WAN videoconference.

Computer-based videoconferencing technology is evolving rapidly. Asynchronous Transfer Mode (ATM) is a new type of network capable of carrying voice, video and computer data. It promises to improve the quality and flexibility of desktop videoconferencing connections.

My desktop system can connect to:

☐ Other computers throughout the organization

☐ Other computers in my department

☐ Our conference room system

☐ A WAN

VIDEOCONFERENCING EQUIPMENT

This section will coach you through learning what you need to know about your videoconferencing equipment. It's important that you know some basics about your system, because they affect what you can do in your meetings.

If you are using a public room, you should read through this section anyway; it will help you speak knowledgeably about your needs as you make arrangements for your meeting.

Who is the best person to teach me about our system?

Name: _____

Title: _____

Location: _____

Phone: _____

INTEROPERABILITY

The International Telecommunications Union has defined a standard, known as *T.120*, for the exchange of data and graphic images among personal computers, videoconferencing systems and peripherals. If your system or equipment does not comply with the T.120 standard, you may experience compatibility problems either within your system and peripherals or in your connections to systems at other sites.

Does our system comply with the T.120 standard?

☐ Yes

☐ No

☐ To some extent

Equipment that *does* meet T.120 standard:

1. _____

2. _____

3. _____

Equipment that *does not* meet T.120 standard:

1. _____

2. _____

3. _____

Cameras

Camera capabilities and placement determine what video images you can transmit to other sites.

A room system usually has one camera in a fixed position to capture a group shot, while others pan, tilt or zoom for details. An auxiliary camera in the rear of the room can focus on a white board or flip chart. Room systems often use *presets*, programmable camera positions that you store and select with the touch of a button. *Voice-activated* cameras are linked to microphones to focus automatically on whomever is speaking. Room systems also have a *document camera* positioned over the table to transmit video images of documents or objects.

Portable systems include at least one camera, usually with pan, tilt and/or zoom capability to capture the room image. Many portable systems can also incorporate auxiliary and document cameras.

Desktop system cameras are mounted on the monitor or on the desk. They are designed to frame one or two people and may have a limited range of focus. Since documents and graphics are transmitted directly from the computer, there is no need for a document camera with a desktop system.

VIDEOCONFERENCING EQUIPMENT (continued)

1. What kind of camera(s) do we have?

   ☐ Room

   ☐ Auxiliary

   ☐ Voice-activated

   ☐ Document

2. How many presets can we program? _____

3. How large a page can the document camera accommodate? _____

4. What other imaging capabilities do we have?

   ☐ Touch-sensitive screen: draw directly on the screen with your finger

   ☐ Freeze-frame: capture video frames as:

      ☐ Bit-mapped graphics

      ☐ Slides

   ☐ Retrieve and display presentation files and bit-mapped graphics from a personal computer

   ☐ People at different sites can manipulate graphics

(Audio Systems)

While the immediate appeal of videoconferencing is the addition of a video image to voice communication, audio quality is more important than image quality. It's better to lose video and still have clear sound than to lose audio and have to complete your meeting with hand-scribbled notes shoved under the document camera!

If you're using a desktop system in an open-office environment, a headphone or handset rather than desktop microphone or speakerphone will help screen out ambient noise.

Check off the type(s) of microphones that you have with your system.

☐ *Ceiling Mics:* set in a fixed position so that everyone at the conference table will be heard clearly.

☐ *Table Mics:* either fixed or portable. Portable table microphones will have to be positioned to get the best and most complete sound coverage. Some experimentation will probably be necessary.

    ☐ *Unidirectional mics* have a narrow pickup zone

    ☐ *Omnidirectional mics* are like a fish-eye lens, gathering audio signals from as wide a range as possible

☐ *Lapel Mics:* lavaliere (wired) or wireless.

☐ *Desktop Systems* may use a:

    ☐ Microphone built into the system

    ☐ Table mic

    ☐ Speakerphone

    ☐ Headset

    ☐ Regular telephone connection

VIDEOCONFERENCING EQUIPMENT
(continued)

Monitors

Room systems usually use a *line monitor* to display the image coming in from other sites, and a *preview monitor* to display the outgoing video. The preview monitor can be used to check an image or graphic before transmitting to other sites. Sometimes a separate *graphics monitor* is part of the system.

Portable systems have one or two monitors. With single-monitor systems, the preview image appears as a small window in the corner of the incoming line image, which uses the full height and width of the screen.

Desktop systems use the computer monitor. Two or more windows display different kinds of information, such as a system document and the image transmitted from the camera at the other end.

SPLIT SCREEN CAPABILITY

A room or portable system camera can comfortably frame three people seated side by side at a conference table. With two cameras and a split screen device, however, it is possible to transmit a composite image of six people at once.

Here's how it works. Each of the two cameras frames three of the six people. The split screen device electronically isolates a central horizontal section of each picture. Since the top part of each picture is the back wall of the room, and the bottom part is the conference table, you don't lose any important information.

These two half-height pictures, each showing three people, are stacked and sent to remote sites as one image. If a remote site has only one monitor, the stacked image is displayed, showing two rows of people one above the other.

If a remote site has two monitors, they can display these two images side by side. The system replaces the missing top and bottom parts of the images with solid black.

1. What type of monitors do we have?

   ☐ Line monitor   ☐ Preview monitor   ☐ Graphics monitor

2. Do we have picture-in-picture capability?   ☐ yes   ☐ no

3. How many windows can I display at one time? _____

4. Can I manipulate the monitor windows?   ☐ yes   ☐ no

5. Do we have split-screen capability?

   ☐ Single monitor   ☐ Dual monitor

VIDEOCONFERENCING EQUIPMENT (continued)

Peripherals

A wide range of peripheral equipment can be connected to videoconferencing systems to expand imaging and other capabilities. Check off the peripheral equipment that is incorporated in your videoconferencing system.

☐ *Personal computer* linked to room or portable system

☐ *High-resolution graphics camera:* when you need more detail than the document camera provides

☐ *Flatbed scanner* (color or monochrome): send the image of a hard copy original at higher resolution than with the document camera

☐ *Fax machine:* send a hard copy image to remote sites during your meeting

☐ *Laser printer:* produce hard copy of images received through the system

☐ *Electronic whiteboard:* use a *tablet* and *stylus* to "draw" on a document on screen

☐ *Audio recorder:* to make a recording of the audio portion of your meeting

☐ *Video recorder:* to make a videotape record of your meeting

Codec

The heart of the videoconferencing system is the codec, short for "coder/decoder." The codec turns sounds and images into digital data and compresses it for transmission. The receiving codec decompresses and decodes the digital data back into sound and picture.

The codec saves time by transmitting only those parts of the image that have changed significantly since the previous frame. This means that:

▶ Minimal movement creates minimal image changes. The codec can compress and code the data quickly, and the resulting image appears to move fairly smoothly.

▶ Broad gestures force the codec to code and compress a great deal of information. When too much information comes in, the codec discards a few frames of image data to stay in real time. This results in a choppy image on the receiving end.

What make and model codec do we use? _____

Inverse Multiplexer

An inverse multiplexer combines several phone channels for greater bandwidth, which means greater capacity and higher resolution audio and video quality. Your receive sites must also have inverse multiplexers with matching capabilities.

1. Do we have an inverse multiplexer?   ☐ yes   ☐ no

2. How many channels can we combine? _____

3. For how much total bandwidth? _____

VIDEOCONFERENCING EQUIPMENT (continued)

Bridge/MCU

The multipoint control unit (MCU) usually referred to as the *bridge,* enables you to connect to more than one other site at a time. The bridge for your system may be on-site, or it may be located at your long-distance carrier.

Since transmitting multiple video and audio signals to multiple sites simultaneously is not yet feasible, the bridge *switches* between sites. Switching gives you the flexibility to view a document from one site while you are hearing commentary from a different site.

Some bridges allow you to add one or more audio-only participants via a regular phone call. They won't receive or transmit any video images, but the rest of you will be able to hear them, and they'll be able to hear you.

1. How many remote sites can I link up at one time?

2. What connecting arrangements does our bridge support?

   ☐ *Meet-me:* other sites call me

   ☐ *Dial-out:* our bridge calls other sites

   ☐ *Hybrid:* meet-me and dial-out combined

3. Can frequently connected sites be speed-dialed? ☐ yes ☐ no

4. Can I can add or drop a site after the conference has begun? ☐ yes ☐ no

5. Can I add voice-only participants? ☐ yes ☐ no How many? _____

6. Which switching modes do we have?

   ☐ *Director control:* one person with a *control unit* controls the switching.

   ☐ *Voice-activation:* the audio signal activates the video signal switch. In other words, whoever's speaking is seen on screen at the receive sites. (The send site continues to see their most recent received image.)

☐ *Rotation:* the video image cycles through the sites displaying each one in turn.

☐ *Self-selection:* someone wishing to become the send site pushes a button to signal the MCU to switch the video source to his/her location.

System Control Unit

The *control unit* is the all-important key pad that puts you in the pilot's seat. It enables you to:

- Dial up your remote sites

- Select and control cameras

- Select incoming video from among remote sites

- Control who's got the microphone

- Adjust audio volume

- Switch to peripherals such as fax machine, VCR, etc.

The control unit for a portable system may not offer as many functions, or as much control, as the control unit for a room system. The control unit for a desktop system is usually a mouse-driven menu, so all you have to do is point and click.

Running a videoconference without knowing how to use the control unit is like trying to fly a plane without knowing what all those buttons and dials on the control panel are for.

SECRET TO SUCCESS

Take the time to master your system's control unit. If you aren't in control of the control unit, you won't be in control of the meeting.

S E C T I O N

III

Balancing Purpose, People and Sites

DETERMINING YOUR PURPOSE

Planning a meeting without knowing your purpose is like packing for vacation without knowing where you are going—should you take ski equipment or a bathing suit? Attending a meeting without a clearly defined purpose is like sitting on the beach in your ski parka. You're not sure why you are there and you wish you were somewhere else.

Planning your videoconference meeting around a clear purpose will avoid having frustrated participants ask themselves "Why are we here?"

The purpose of my meeting is to:

☐ Share information about: _____

☐ Set goals for: _____

☐ Make a decision about: _____

☐ Solve the problem of: _____

Set a Specific Objective

Your objective is the specific outcome you want to achieve by the end of your videoconference: *"At the conclusion of this videoconference we will have . . ."*

> *". . . reviewed the results of the Chicago and St. Louis focus groups."* [shared information]

> *". . . established target dates for each phase of the project."* [set goals]

> *". . . outlined the elements of our business development strategy."* [made a decision]

> *". . . agreed on a procedure for handling excess inventory."* [solved a problem]

Write your objective as a statement:

"At the conclusion of this videoconference, we will have _____

_____

_____ ."

WHO SHOULD ATTEND

The purpose of your meeting will help you determine who should attend and how many sites can be incorporated effectively.

Information Sharing

SITES: A large number of locations will not be a problem, as long as little discussion is expected.

PEOPLE: You may be able to include everyone with whom you wish to share your information, or you can include a representative from each group of people who need to be informed.

Goal Setting

SITES: When the meeting will involve a lot of discussion, keep the number of sites to a minimum.

PEOPLE: Involve those people whose needs and objectives will determine the goals to be set. Consider also people whose input will help you achieve time-sensitive goals.

Decision Making

SITES: If the decision will be made jointly, keep the number of sites small. If you are gathering information to make a decision yourself, more sites can be managed.

PEOPLE: Include people whose input you need to make your decision or who will share responsibility for a joint decision.

Problem Solving

SITES: Solving a problem requires the most interaction and is hardest to manage in a multipoint meeting. Problem solving is best accomplished in a point-to-point meeting between two sites, although three or even four sites are possible.

PEOPLE: Include those people who share responsibility for solving the problem, as well as people who can help you:

✔ identify root causes

✔ propose alternative solutions

✔ help you evaluate the feasibility of your proposed solution(s)

SPECIAL GUESTS CAN ADD IMPACT TO YOUR VIDEOCONFERENCE

SPECIAL GUESTS

One great advantage of videoconferencing is that more people can join in your meeting. A brief presentation from a senior executive can add a lot of impact—and it will take only a few minutes of her time.

Sometimes you just need to discuss a project with a colleague. For other videoconference meetings, you may want to ask for participation from:

✔ *Senior Managers or Executives*—especially if your meeting concerns rolling out a new product, strategy or policy.

I may want to include: _____

_____

_____

✔ *Subject Matter Experts* from other locations within or outside the organization—especially if you're exploring alternative solutions and their possible impact.

I may want to include: _____

_____

_____

✔ *Stakeholders* who can affect, or who will be affected by, your decisions—especially if the topics to be discussed are controversial.

I may want to include: _____

_____

_____

✔ *Customers or Suppliers* who can provide input for your decisions—especially where product quality is a concern.

I may want to include: _____

_____

_____

Use the worksheet below to develop a complete list of sites and participants for your videoconference meeting.

Videoconference Participation

SITE	PARTICIPANTS
1.	
2.	
3.	
4.	
5.	
6.	

EVALUATING COSTS AND SAVINGS

If meeting with Carla in Dallas by videoconferencing will save you the time and expense of a trip, go for it! Sometimes, however, you'll want to do a detailed cost analysis. Say you want to connect eight people in eight regional offices, none of which has its own videoconferencing equipment. Your costs will include public room rental in each city. It may be more cost effective to have some people travel to combine sites. The following diagram illustrates one possibility; combining eight people at eight sites to eight people at four sites.

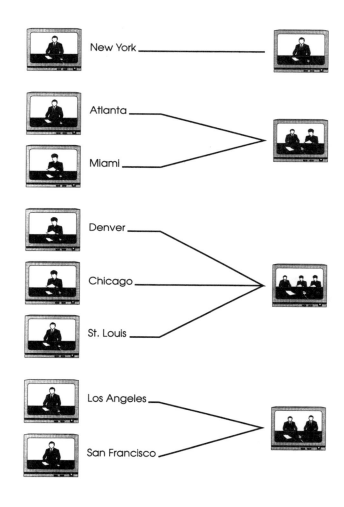

New York

Atlanta

Miami

Denver

Chicago

St. Louis

Los Angeles

San Francisco

COST COMPARISON

Use the worksheets on the following pages to estimate the cost of your video-conference. Keep in mind that it may save money to have another site make the connect-up calls, especially for an international conference. These worksheets are repeated in the TOOLS section at the back of the book.

IN-PERSON MEETING		
Salaries	Meeting time and travel time for all participants	$
Benefits, taxes	35%–50% of salary. Check with personnel department	$
Travel costs	Mileage	$
	Tolls	$
	Parking	$
	Airfare	$
	Rental cars/taxi	$
	Food	$
	Lodging	$
Room Charge	Cost of hotel meeting room (if applicable)	$
TOTAL		$

COST COMPARISON (continued)

VIDEOCONFERENCE MEETING		
Salaries	Meeting time for all participants, plus travel time to videoconferencing sites, if other than the office	$
Benefits, taxes	Use same percentage as for in-person meeting	$
Travel costs (to videoconferencing sites, if other than office)	Mileage	$
	Tolls	$
	Parking	$
	Airfare	$
	Rental cars/taxi	$
	Food	$
	Lodging	$
Network access	Cost to hook up to your carrier	$
Network usage	Long distance phone charges	$
	Usage fee for public switched network	$
Room charge	Total cost per hour for any public rooms, times length of meeting	$
TOTAL COST		$

SECRET TO SUCCESS

An effective videoconference is focused and productive. Use your purpose statement as a guiding light throughout the planning process.

SECTION

IV

Planning Your Meeting

YOUR PLANNING STYLE

Check the description below that most matches how you prepare to lead a meeting.

☐ **#1** I spend a few minutes thinking about how I'll start things off and jotting down a few notes about what I'd like to cover. Then I play it by ear—I've run so many meetings I could do it in my sleep.

☐ **#2** I write down my issues and note any strong priorities. I review my agenda orally at the beginning of the meeting. We usually don't get through everything on my list, so I try to tackle the most important stuff first.

☐ **#3** I try to plan everything at least a few days in advance, so I can send the agenda out beforehand. Along with the agenda, I often send a request for participants to do some preparation so we can spend more time making decisions and less time talking in circles.

If you checked #1, you're a *seat-of-the-pants* meeting leader. We'd like to congratulate you on getting anything at all accomplished in your meetings! Clear a little extra room on your schedule for planning your videoconference.

If you checked #2, you're *semi-organized* and off to a good start. However, you'll need to expand your planning activities if your videoconference is to be a success. The following pages will show you how.

If you checked #3, you're an *accomplished* planner. No matter how many face-to-face meetings you may have run, however, your first videoconference will take some extra planning to avoid potential pitfalls.

PREPARING YOUR STORYBOARD

The success of a videoconference meeting is in the details. The storyboard is a map of your videoconference meeting, which enables you to:

- Plan all the details of your meeting in one place
- Vary the pace of interaction
- Make sure you have all the support materials you need
- Manage the equipment while you are leading discussions or delegate system operation to someone else
- Ensure that your videoconference is focused and productive
- Keep the meeting on track and on schedule

Storyboard Format

Your storyboard has six vertical columns, as shown in the example at the bottom of these two pages. A full-size blank storyboard is provided in the TOOLS section at the back of the book for you to photocopy and use, or you can set up a storyboard format with your word processing software and create the meeting plan on your computer.

STORYBOARD FOR: Jan. 8th Regional Manager's meeting

TIME	TOPIC	CONTENT/METHOD
2:15–2:20	Last quarter's results	Review results vs. goal
2:20–2:30		Regional sites present reasons for success/shortfall
2:30–2:50		Lead discussion on problems and potential solutions
(3)	(1)	(2)

(1) **TOPIC:** Use this column to identify the major topics you'll cover in your meeting.

(2) **CONTENT/METHOD:** Use this column to define content and interaction for each topic, such as open discussion, small group brainstorming, etc.

(3) **TIME:** After planning content and interaction, you'll be able to estimate how long each topic will take to complete and what the time should be at each stage of your meeting. This information is on the far left side so it will be easy to see at a glance during the meeting.

(4) **SUPPORT:** Use this column to record all the support materials you plan to use for each topic: handouts, graphics, computer files, etc.

(5) **SYSTEM CUES:** Use this column to record instructions for operating the videoconferencing system controls: using the graphics camera, switching to voice-activation mode, etc.

(6) **PARTICIPATION:** Use this column during the videoconference to track remote site participation. List sites and participants here.

Page: _____ **of** _____

SUPPORT	SYSTEM CUES	PARTICIPATION	
Tables 3 and 4	Director control Document camera	Minneapolis	Anne Lafrey Mark Cohen Sarah Martin
	Voice-activated	Seattle	Ed Woodson Phil Jacobs Pat Laramy
		Phoenix	Mitch Fields Dave Dunby Abbie Millar
(4)	**(5)**	**(6)**	

PREPARING YOUR STORYBOARD (continued)

Developing the Storyboard

For a long or complex videoconference meeting, you may find it helpful to use a separate storyboard page for each topic.

If you plan to put more than one topic on a page, work on one topic at a time before moving on. Then draw a line across the page and begin the next topic below the line. This way you'll be sure to have enough room to record all the pertinent details for each topic. Be sure to number your pages.

Step-by-step instructions for using the storyboard to plan your videoconference meeting begin below.

Column 1: Topic

1. Develop Topics List

List the major issues you'll need to address to achieve your objective. Include welcoming remarks and a site check to make sure everyone is properly hooked up.

☐ *Welcome and site check.* _____

☐ _____

☐ _____

2. Plan Premeeting Work

Review your topic list for items that can be prepared or completed in advance by you or someone else. For example, you might ask participants at each site to hold a local brainstorming session before the videoconference to come up with possible solutions to a problem. Include any premeeting work that will be reviewed during the meeting on your topic list.

3. Plan Postconference Activities

After the videoconference, the local group at each site can hold a follow-up discussion or action planning session while they are all together. Include this on your topics list, so you can plan to review postconference session objectives and follow-up procedures before you go "off the air."

4. Determine Sequence

When your list is complete, number the topics in a logical sequence, using the boxes provided.

5. Storyboard Topic #1

Write your first topic on the storyboard, then go on to column 2.

Column 2: Content/Method

1. Identify Specific Content for Your Topic

- Information that you or someone else will present
- Issues that will require discussion
- A decision to be made

2. Decide on Method

On your storyboard, describe each content item and method in an action phrase. Indicate specific remote sites where appropriate. For example:

Sheila Broome (Seattle) presents results of November focus groups

Lead a discussion on root causes of the problem

Ask for input from Denver on customer priorities in their area

3. Review for Interaction and Variety

As you plan your content and methods, keep an eye on the overall pace of the meeting and build in variety. Use these tips to help generate ideas.

- Conduct some kind of interaction as early in the meeting as possible, so people don't fall into a passive, "watching TV" mentality.
- Get a discussion going between two remote sites, so participants don't feel that everything has to go through you.
- Prepare a question or two related to each topic. If discussion lags, you'll be ready with a pertinent question to get things moving again.
- Display a graphic and ask for comments. A visual image, such as a chart or diagram, is a good way to stimulate discussion.

PREPARING YOUR STORYBOARD (continued)

4. Take Advantage of Remote-Site Groups

Participants gathered at each site can work as a small group. Brainstorming in particular is better suited to small groups than to a multipoint discussion. After each site has shared ideas or opinions, circulate these to each of the other sites for feedback and discussion.

For remote-site activities, make sure everyone understands:

- The objective to be accomplished (generate a list of points, come up with a potential solution to a problem, etc.)

- Time allotted for remote site discussion

- How and when results will be shared

Column 3: Time

Accurate scheduling is essential when planning a videoconference. If you are using a public room, running overtime will be either impossible or expensive. Even in your own organization if you're booked until 2:00, someone else may be waiting in the hall by 1:55 to dial up another conference.

1. Estimate How Long Each Topic Will Take

- *Information sharing* usually goes quickly; each person takes a turn, and there is minimal discussion.

- *Goal setting* often involves a lot more discussion, especially if people have different priorities.

- *Decision making*—Are you going to make the decision yourself, or is the decision to be a joint one? Joint decisions take longer.

- *Problem solving* requires the most interaction, since meeting participants suggest alternatives, weigh pros and cons, discuss alternatives, etc.

It takes longer to get feedback from eight participants divided among four sites than from eight participants grouped at two sites. Presentation time is easier to estimate than discussion and decision time. Allow a little extra time in case discussions or decisions take longer than expected.

2. Calculate Elapsed Time

If the meeting is not yet scheduled, calculate how long the meeting will have run at the conclusion of each topic. If the meeting has been scheduled, determine what the time should be at that point in the meeting.

3. Evaluate Meeting Length

If your meeting will run more than 90 minutes, go back to your storyboard and include a five- to 10-minute break. If your time estimates show that your videoconference will run longer than the time available, you can choose to:

- Cut one or more topics
- Revise your methods to incorporate less discussion
- Use pre- or postmeeting work
- Rethink your site/participant list
- Plan more than one meeting

Column 4: Support

In column 4, record all the support materials you plan to use for each topic, such as handouts, visuals and videotapes.

1. Handouts

- Include references to prepared handouts and/or reading (such as a quarterly report) that participants were asked to do before the meeting.
- If possible, mail, modem or fax handouts to all sites before the meeting. Handouts can also be faxed to remote sites during the meeting.
- Desktop systems can display the appropriate file to all sites, so you may not need hard copies of handouts.

PREPARING YOUR STORYBOARD (continued)

2. Visuals

If your meeting will have long stretches of presentation, bullet lists, charts and diagrams will be important to keeping participants awake and interested. Follow these guidelines for effective visuals.

- Keep bullet lists simple

    —No more than three or four bullet points or six lines per screen

    —Use large, simple fonts and upper and lower case letters rather than all caps

    —Put details in a handout

- Number each visual (slide #1, diagram B), rather than relying on a description such as "chart of year-end results."

3. Computer-Generated Graphics

Presentation graphics programs enable you to produce colorful charts, diagrams and bullet lists in minutes. Keep these three important issues in mind.

1. *Aspect ratio:* Videoconferencing monitors are four units high and three units wide. This is an aspect ratio of 4:3. Your presentation graphics program default settings may not match this. If your system allows you to display 35 mm slides, they must be in landscape (horizontal) format in order to fit the aspect ratio.

2. *Safe margins:* The monitor case covers the edges of the picture tube. Use a margin of 10%–15% of the image size on all your graphics.

3. *Technical issues:*

    - If you are using a desktop system, displaying computer-generated graphics will be no problem. With a room or portable system, you may need a video scan converter to display graphics directly from your computer.

    - If necessary, you can print graphics with a color printer and display them as hard copy via the document camera.

    - Video monitor resolution is much lower than computer monitor resolution. Preview a representative graphic on the system to check for legibility limitations.

4. Hand-Written Notes

- Use an $8^1/_2" \times 11"$ sheet of paper, in landscape position, and the document camera instead of a flip chart or white board. The flip chart's vertical format won't fit the monitor's aspect ratio, and whiteboards often cause glare or reflections.

- Avoid smooth white paper such as that designed for use in laser printers, since it is reflective and can cause glare. Use pastel or off-white paper and a blue fat-tip pen.

- Print in large block letters, and leave a safe margin of $1^1/_2"–2"$ on all sides.

5. Videotapes

A prerecorded videotape can be a great addition to your videoconference, as long as you keep these issues in mind.

1. *Compression:* Movement on a videotape causes the same compression problems as live movement in the meeting room.

2. *Quality:* Audio and signal quality of prerecorded tapes vary tremendously. Preview tapes on the system before deciding whether or not to use them.

3. *Copyright issues:* A rented videotape may be licensed for use at one site only. Make sure you have permission to display it to other sites, especially if you plan to make a videotape of your meeting.

4. *Attention spans:* Too much video can be as sleep-inducing as too much talk. Short (five-minute) segments are best.

INFORMATION ON SYSTEMS CUES

PREPARING YOUR STORYBOARD (continued)

Column 5: System Cues

Use this column to record instructions for operating the system controls, including switching mode, document cameras, VCRs, etc. Issues to keep in mind include:

1. Switching Mode

Be aware of the trade-off between how much attention you can give to the meeting and how much attention you can give to the system.

- *Voice-activated mode* allows you to pay more attention to the meeting
- *Director control mode* will take your attention away from the meeting unless you have delegated the control unit to someone else

2. Displaying Graphics

- Transparencies can be displayed via the document camera. Place a sheet of pastel-colored paper behind black and white transparencies.
- When you use the graphics buffer in a dual-monitor system, your graphic can remain on-screen while the video switches around among sites.
- If an image won't fit under the document camera, it can be taped to a wall or flip chart and displayed through one of the room cameras.

3. Recording Your Meeting

A videotape record of your meeting may come in handy at a later date to clarify questions that might arise or to help resolve a dispute about a contract or negotiation. Long-term projects also benefit from a videotape library of project meetings. As personnel change, new team members can be brought up to speed quickly about the project's history and direction and who the players are.

Videotapes may also be used to keep a broader audience informed about company events. If you plan to use your meeting record for this purpose, you will probably want to produce an edited highlights version.

Keep these issues in mind if you plan to record your meeting.

- Unless you have two VCRs, you will not be able to tape your meeting and show a prerecorded tape at the same time. Depending on your system and meeting configuration, you may be able to tape the meeting from another site and show the video segment from your site (or vice versa).

- If graphics are displayed on a separate graphics monitor (rather than the line monitor), they won't be captured by your videotape. You can get around this by transmitting the graphics in place of the live camera image from your site—although this means that your audience will not be able to see you and your graphics at the same time.

- When you make a videotape record of your meeting, you will be taping the incoming video channel plus the audio from all sites. If you have an additional VCR set up, you can record your outgoing video on that machine. You'll then have two tapes, which can be edited together. This provides a good opportunity to edit out nonsignificant moments and add additional graphics.

Column 6: Participation

You will use this column during the videoconference to track remote site participation. (We'll show you how later in the book.) For now, prepare this section of your storyboard by listing all participants, by site, for each topic.

PREPARING A "TO DO" LIST

Once you have completed your storyboard, use it to develop a detailed list of everything you need to do to prepare for your meeting. Use this page to start your "to do" list.

☐ Preparing your visuals _____

_____

☐ Sending out advance reading, such as a quarterly sales report, to all participants _____

_____

☐ Preparing and distributing any handouts you plan to use during the meeting _____

_____

☐ Determining availability of support materials, such as renting that 10-minute videotape on calming upset customers _____

_____

☐ Making sure you will have a specific product or piece of equipment on hand

_____

☐ Communicating with participants who are responsible for preparing prework _____

_____

☐ Arranging for special guests, such as finding out if Pam is available to give a brief presentation on the new product launch _____

_____

SECRET TO SUCCESS

Staff at remote sites must feel like participants, not an audience—careful planning is essential to effective interaction.

S E C T I O N

V

Getting Ready

SCHEDULING THE MEETING

Scheduling your videoconference for a time when everyone can be there and all the sites are available could be your biggest headache.

Public rooms must be scheduled in advance. If you are booking for a peak time period (that section of the day when business hours in different time zones overlap), more than a week's notice may be necessary.

For room and portable system users, your first step is to find out who is in charge of scheduling videoconferences in your department or organization. Companies with many videoconferencing locations usually have a site coordinator or administrator responsible for scheduling. If you will be coordinating and confirming times yourself, find out what your company's policies and procedures are and be sure to follow them.

Scheduling software may be integrated into your videoconferencing system. Sprint, AT&T and MCI all offer on-line scheduling tools to their videoconferencing customers. These services enable you to coordinate multiple sites serviced by the same carrier for automatic connection at your scheduled time.

SCHEDULING THE MEETING (continued)

Time Zones

If you are scheduling across time zones, make doubly, triply, quadruply sure that everyone involved knows which time zone's time you are talking about. Remember that daylight savings time comes and goes in some countries. What was a nine-hour time difference for your last meeting might be a ten-hour (or eight-hour) difference this time.

For videoconferences that span multiple time zones, setting an appropriate time for the meeting can be a challenge.

Finding a window when people in both Washington, D.C. and Los Angeles will be at work isn't too difficult: An early afternoon call from the east coast will be a morning connection in Los Angeles.

► If the Washington, D.C. connection is to Sydney, Australia, it gets a little more complex:

- A 9:00 a.m. call from Joe in Washington will reach Arlene in Sydney at midnight local time.

- If Arlene places the 9:00 a.m. call, it will reach Joe at 6:00 p.m. the previous day.

► If Martine and Claude in Paris are participating, they'll be propping their eyes open at midnight waiting for the connection to come through from Australia. They'd rather have the call come in from Joe at 3:00 p.m. (9:00 a.m. in Washington), and make Arlene stay up.

SCHEDULING HEADACHES AND WHAT YOU CAN DO ABOUT THEM

HEADACHE: You've worked out three possible times to hold a multi-time zone videoconference at reasonably convenient hours for everyone involved, but the conference room isn't available for any of those time slots.

ASPIRIN: Find out who's signed up for the room at the time you want it, and ask if they can reschedule or relocate. You also may be able to negotiate for the use of another department's videoconferencing equipment.

HEADACHE: Your videoconference is scheduled to begin at 2:00 p.m., but when you show up at 1:50 to set up your stuff, someone else is still using the room.

ASPIRIN: Find out ahead of time how much "cushion" time (if any) is provided between meeting time slots. If you can't get into the room until 2:00, consider scheduling your meeting for 2:10 or 2:15. This will give you time to confirm connections and get your materials set up.

HEADACHE: Your videoconference is scheduled for 2:00 p.m. today. At 10:30 a.m. the big cheese's secretary calls to say he's going to be using the conference room all afternoon and you'll have to make other plans.

ASPIRIN: Find out ahead of time what the company policy is on use of the room. If there's a chance you'll be bumped by a more senior user, even one who isn't using the videoconferencing equipment, make back-up plans.

HEADACHE: You'll be holding regular weekly meetings with your counterparts in the Europe and Far East offices, and no matter when you schedule the meetings, someone will have to stay up late.

ASPIRIN: Vary connect times so different sites take turns staying up late, or ask people what would suit their body clock. Sue might prefer to meet at midnight her time once a week than ever have to be awake, alert and dressed for business at 6:00 a.m. Jim, who's up with the roosters every morning, might be so tired and cranky by midnight that his participation would be only marginally useful.

PREMEETING CORRESPONDENCE

Every participant should get a letter about the meeting at least several days in advance—longer if any preparation is involved. This letter should provide:

☐ A list of who will be attending, at what sites

☐ The meeting purpose and objective

☐ An overview of key topics and time frames (from your storyboard)

☐ Details about any premeeting work to be done (e.g., review a report, compile a list of top customer complaints about a product; come up with three ideas for how to cut response time, etc.)

☐ A reminder to be on time

☐ Videoconferencing guidelines, and a request to review them. (A sample guidelines memo is provided on the following pages.)

Your cover letter to participants can include information similar to the following:

I look forward to your participation in our videoconference on January 18th at 7 p.m. EST. Please take a moment to review the enclosed guidelines before the meeting.

MAKE SURE EACH PARTICIPANT HAS A COPY OF THE GUIDELINES

VIDEOCONFERENCING GUIDELINES

Appearance

Clothes

Do wear
- A simple, tailored suit or dress in a medium-dark color. Royal blue, purple and burgundy are good choices for women, blue or charcoal gray for men.
- Solid, rather than patterned fabrics.
- Pastel shirt or blouse, rather than white.

Avoid
- Bright red, white or black.
- Bold plaids or complicated patterns.
- Scarves, ruffles and rustly fabrics.
- Clothes that match the color of the conference room walls.

Makeup and Grooming

Avoid
- Dark or very bright lipsticks.
- Dark eyeshadows.
- Strong blush.
- A hair style that will tempt you to fuss with it, such as bangs that fall into your eyes.

Accessories

Do
- Keep accessories to a minimum.
- Bring an extra necktie if you're not sure what will look good on camera.

Avoid
- Reflective accessories such as brooches, tie clasps, large earrings.
- Dangly or noisy bracelets or necklaces.
- Tinted eyeglass lenses, if you have a choice.

VIDEOCONFERENCING GUIDELINES

Participation

Do
- Ask questions, make comments and share your knowledge.

- Identify yourself when you speak: "This is Sue in Atlanta, and I'd like to comment on . . ."

- Speak with a normal tone and volume. The microphones are sensitive, so there is no need to lean toward the mic when speaking or to raise your voice.

- You will notice a slight delay in audio transmission:

  —When you are speaking, pause longer than usual to allow others to respond before you go on.
  —When someone else is speaking, wait to make sure he or she has finished before you respond.

- Look at the monitor while speaking, rather than at the table or at other people in the room.

- Leave your microphone on mute until the meeting starts.

- Relax and enjoy the meeting.

Avoid
- Making noises that will be picked up and amplified by the microphones. This includes:

  —Shuffling papers.
  —Drumming your fingers.
  —Tapping a pen or pencil.
  —Banging water carafes, glasses, coffee cups and silverware on the table. A water glass set down on a hard surface may go unnoticed at your end and sound like a hammer blow at remote sites.

- Side conversations with other people in the room. If the mics are open, everyone will hear you.

- Adjusting the microphones once the meeting starts, except to turn the mute function on and off. If another location cannot hear you, they need to turn their room control volume up.

- Moving around a lot if your chair swivels or has casters.

- Using overly active gestures, since these may cause the outgoing video image to become choppy.

SETTING UP THE ROOM

You may be one of the fortunate few using a professionally designed videoconferencing room where everything is just right. More likely, the videoconferencing equipment has been stashed in whatever conference room was available. Lighting, seating arrangements and sound quality may be less than ideal, and your ability to adjust the problem factors may be limited. If you are using a desktop system, you're probably stuck with your office environment as it is.

Use the general tips below (and the lighting, camera and sound checklists on the following pages) to make your environment as good as it can be.

Eight Tips for Setting Up the Room

1. Rooms with lots of white and/or dark colors create problems with the camera's white balance, which can result in unnatural-looking skin tones.

2. If you have poorly shaded windows, a distracting background wall or a problem with echoes, consider renting a midrange grey or blue photographer's backdrop and hanging it behind the conference table.

3. Avoid boldly patterned carpets or upholstery, if possible.

4. Take down art work if possible, especially on the back wall of the room; glass surfaces and metallic frames can cause reflections and glare.

5. Choose chairs that don't swivel and that are not on casters, so people won't move around too much.

6. All participants should have name tags and/or tent cards, and a table or wall sign identifying the site. Send these out ahead of time, or check that they will be available at remote sites.

- Tent cards will be easier to read than name tags in group shots
- Name tags will be easier to read in close-up shots

7. Each site should have a clearly visible clock so that participants remain aware of the time.

8. If you are using a wireless control unit, *make sure you have back-up batteries.* Find out if you have back-up mechanical control available if necessary, and learn how to use it.

SETTING UP THE ROOM (continued)

Lighting

What You Want:

► Lighting that produces an image with balanced contrast, effective shadows and highlights and a comfortable environment

► Multiple light sources evenly distributed throughout the room

► Cool white or blue-white fluorescent bulbs in overhead fixtures

► An area of shadow for the monitors, so the picture is easy to see

What You Might Have:

► Overhead lights that reflect off bald heads and create unattractive shadows under eyebrows, noses and chins

► Hot bright lights that trigger a noisy air-conditioning system

► Low lighting that washes out colors and creates prominent shadows

► Warm-yellow lights that make people look jaundiced and cause flicker on the video image

► Lights that cause glare, reflections and a washed-out image on the monitors

What You Can Do:

☐ Make sure lights are not pointing at the cameras or monitors

☐ Sit in each seat that will be used during your meeting, to check for:

- Light shining in your eyes

- Unflattering facial shadows (use the preview monitor)

- Shadows on the table in front of you that will make papers difficult to read

☐ Light the back wall to create a good contrast in the participant image

☐ If the conference table has a highly reflective finish, cover it with a table cloth to reduce glare

☐ If light levels are too low, put a light-colored or white table cloth on the table to reflect some light into the room and onto faces

Camera Positions

What You Want:

► Cameras placed above or below the main monitor so you'll appear to be looking directly into the camera as you watch the screen

► Presets that provide a useful balance of close-up and zoom shots

► Cameras at an appropriate distance from participants

► Graphics and document cameras that are easily accessible

SETTING UP THE ROOM (continued)

What You Might Have:

► Main camera at an angle to the conference table—at remote sites you may appear to be looking off to the side, at something out of camera range

► Presets from a previous meeting that don't suit your seating arrangement

► Cameras limited to a wide angle group shot that results in small figures and lost detail on the remote monitors

► Graphics and document cameras that can't be reached from your seat

What You Can Do:

☐ Consider adjusting the seating arrangements rather than camera placements

☐ Make sure you have presets that will frame a group of two to three people and use these positions (rather than close-ups) during voice-activated switching to avoid excessive camera shifts

☐ In a conference with no more than three participants at each site, consider setting up the cameras for a group shot from each site and using those settings throughout the meeting

☐ Use the preview monitor to check the displayed image from each camera and preset position

☐ Make sure facial expressions and reactions will come through—remember that the monitor at the remote site may be smaller or farther from the table than the one at your end

Sound Systems

What You Want:

- ► One microphone for every two or three participants

- ► Clear, undistorted sound pickup

- ► Microphones placed so that participants can speak naturally

- ► Speakers located next to the monitors so sound and picture appear to come from the same spot

What You Might Have:

- ► Limited microphones in fixed positions

- ► Unidirectional microphones that limit the speaker's range of motion

- ► Wireless lapel microphones that wandered off with the last person to use them

- ► Microphones that pick up a lot of background noise

What You Can Do:

☐ Redistribute microphones in the room, if possible, to suit your meeting

☐ Check sound pickup quality from every location in the room that you are likely to use during your meeting

☐ Test the room microphones while the heating or air-conditioning system is running, and find positions that pick up minimal background noise

☐ Make sure participants at all sites know not to touch the microphones except to activate the mute feature

SEATING ARRANGEMENTS

A good seating arrangement is an important element to the success of your videoconference. It should produce a good on-screen image at remote sites, facilitate discussion by providing a good view of the monitor from every seat and provide an appropriate position for the meeting leader.

The size and shape of your conference table and meeting room will determine possible seating arrangements. The tips below, and the guidelines on the following pages, will help you arrange participant seating most effectively.

Five Tips for Effective Seating

1. Allow each person three feet at the table. A camera 10'–11' from the participants should be able to frame three people comfortably.

2. For videoconferencing use, the average conference table is only comfortable and effective for groups of six or fewer people.

3. Measure the height of your monitor. Viewers should be seated at a distance from the screen that is between four and seven times the height of the monitor.

4. The location of the control unit may affect your meeting dynamics:

- If the control unit is built into the system, it can limit the places the meeting leader can sit

- If your system has a wireless control unit, meeting leadership can be shared among everyone in the room

5. It's better to have people face the camera than each other, to encourage inter-action between sites. When a small group is seated on the same side of the table facing the camera, discussions tend to focus more naturally on remote sites than on the other people in the room. However, in-room discussion becomes difficult.

COMMON SEATING ARRANGEMENTS

Oval Conference Table

The arc of an oval table allows a small group to sit along one side without losing sight of each other as much as at a rectangular table. Apparent on-screen size differences are minimized, as everyone is approximately the same distance from the camera.

Sitting like this

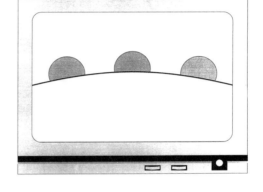

Looks like this on the monitor

In-room conversation is a little difficult with an oval table, though not as bad as a shoulder-to-shoulder arrangement at a rectangular table.

Depending on the size of the table, it can be difficult to seat groups larger than four or five people. Use the preview monitor to see how many people can be accommodated in a group shot—or in a split-screen double shot if you have that capability— then limit the number of on-site participants to match camera capacity.

COMMON SEATING ARRANGEMENTS
(continued)

Square or Rectangular Conference Table

Avoid seating a group on opposing sides of the table. One person may block someone else's view of the monitor, and people are likely to interact more with each other than with remote sites.

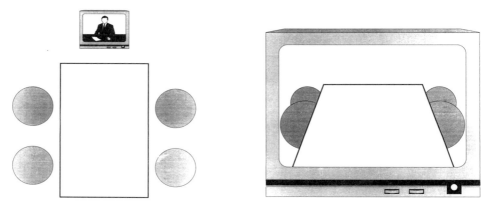

Sitting like this   Looks like this on the monitor

If only three or four people are at the meeting, they can sit along one side of the table, facing the camera for a good group shot. With a larger group, however, it can be difficult to set up a shot that includes everyone.

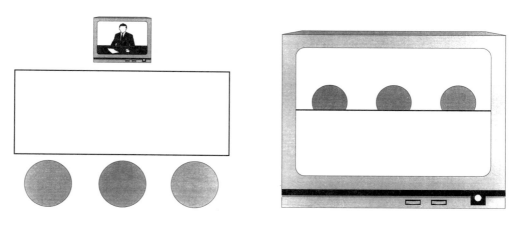

Sitting like this   Looks like this on the monitor

If you are using a portable system, consider positioning it for a diagonal shot of one side and end of the table. This will give everyone a good view of each other and the monitor.

Sitting like this

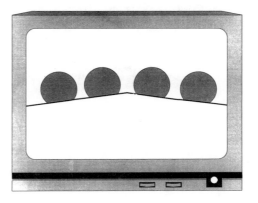

Looks like this on the monitor

IS YOUR TABLE A TRAPEZOID?

COMMON SEATING ARRANGEMENTS
(continued)

Trapezoid Table

This table shape is more common in television studios, where it is used for panel discussion shows, than in office environments. You may have one if your room was designed specifically for videoconferencing.

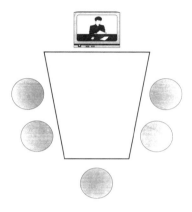

Sitting like this

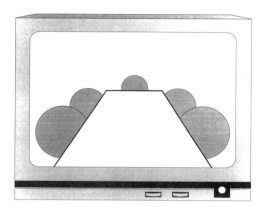

Looks like this on the monitor

When two or three people are seated along each of the angled sides, the on-screen image will have the illusion of everyone seated at a rectangular table. Because in-room discussion is easier, it may detract from between-site discussions.

Avoid placing anyone at the narrow end of the table (farthest from camera), as they will appear small and far away on screen.

SECRET TO SUCCESS

People should come away from your videoconference talking about the meeting, not the technology.

SECTION VI

Leading the Meeting

DO YOU NEED A TECHNICIAN?

If you are using a public room, a technician will make the site connections for you and operate the system throughout your meeting unless you need privacy. If you are not using a public room, use this checklist to help determine if you need a videoconferencing technician on hand. The more "yes" answers you check, the more capable you are of running a meeting on your own.

	YES	NO
1. I know how to connect with my remote sites.	☐	☐
2. I'm doing a point-to-point meeting, so I won't have to worry about switching between sites.	☐	☐
3. I can troubleshoot common problems.	☐	☐
4. I plan to use a minimum of peripherals (scanner, fax, VCR, etc.).	☐	☐
5. I know the other participants well and am not too worried about having to be at my best.	☐	☐
6. I will have the time and attention during the meeting to be managing camera, microphone and switching modes and selections.	☐	☐
7. I won't have the time to handle those things, but someone else at my site can do it.	☐	☐
8. We're on a charge-back system, and I don't have the budget to pay for a technician.	☐	☐
9. I'm expected to muddle through on my own. No technician is available.	☐	☐

OVERCOMING NERVOUSNESS

Running a videoconference for the first time can be both exciting and intimidating. If you feel nervous, you may be reacting to one or more of three main reasons for lack of confidence about leading a videoconference.

Confidence Assessment

Here is a quick assessment and some key actions you can take.

☐ **I don't feel prepared for the meeting agenda.**

- Get other people involved: Ask someone else to lead a portion of the meeting.

- Request that participants come prepared to share ideas, reports.

- Hold a premeeting meeting with key people to get their input and ideas.

☐ **I don't feel prepared to use the equipment.**

- Practice with the equipment if you can.

- Attend someone else's videoconference as an observer. Watch who does what when and how.

- Learn one thing at a time: using the document camera, the preview monitor, the control unit.

- Hold a point-to-point practice meeting with a colleague in another city.

☐ **I don't have confidence in my abilities.**

- Remember a time in the past when you successfully tackled a new situation. Focus on how great your achievement felt.

- Visualize success. Sit quietly with your eyes closed and take a few deep, slow breaths. Now picture yourself conducting a great meeting. Hear people congratulating you for a job well done when it's over. Allow yourself to experience a feeling of deep satisfaction.

- Don't expect to be perfect.

Eight Ways to Increase Your Confidence

1. Learn how to use the equipment, so you are not dependent on someone else. Even if you always have a technician's assistance, this will raise your confidence.

2. Allow yourself enough lead time to plan the meeting thoroughly. Videoconferences do take more planning than an in-person meeting. It's hard to feel confident if you are rushed and underprepared.

3. Go over your storyboard and highlight every time you have "director control" in one color, every time you use document camera in a different color, and so on. Keep in mind that the purpose of this highlighting is to help you practice—don't rely on highlighting alone to guide you through the meeting.

4. Practice following your highlighted storyboard with the equipment: cuing up videotapes, placing documents under the document camera, using the control unit to switch cameras and microphones, etc. Videotape your dry run, so you can review it.

5. Identify specific things that you are afraid of. What's the worst that can happen? Come up with at least one thing you can do to be better prepared for your worst-case scenario. Now make a commitment to yourself that you will do your best, no matter what happens.

6. Release your physical tension. Jump up and down a few times. Take a quick walk down the hall or around the building. Shake out your arms and legs. Roll your head from side to side. Choose some favorite warm-up moves from an exercise video, and take a few moments to work the kinks out.

7. Take several deep, slow breaths. Picture your tension as a dark cloud filling your body; every time you exhale, imagine blowing that cloud out of your system. When you inhale, imagine breathing in clean, bright sunlight.

8. Act confident, even if you have to fake it.

OVERCOMING NERVOUSNESS (continued)

Your Confidence Action Plan

Take a few minutes to choose five key actions that you will take to increase your confidence in leading a videoconference meeting. Assign a target date for completion of each action step.

I will improve my confidence by:

1. _____ by: _____

2. _____ by: _____

3. _____ by: _____

4. _____ by: _____

5. _____ by: _____

FIRST THINGS FIRST

Equipment Check

► Test your system configuration before every meeting

- Heating or air-conditioning that was silent last time may be noisy today.

- If your room has exterior windows, light levels may be very different from day to day, even with the shades drawn.

- Portable systems are sensitive to jostling and jarring. If the system has been moved recently, make sure it is working properly.

► Check that microphones are plugged in and monitors are turned on.

Welcoming Remarks

► Display a welcome visual as remote sites come on line. Include the date, a description of the meeting, origination site and participating sites.

► Introduce yourself if necessary, then introduce any other participants at your site. Also introduce support staff or observers present during the meeting and mention their roles.

► Switch the camera to each remote site in turn. Call on someone by name at each site to start the introductions: "We have a group from the Boston office joining us today. Martin, would you begin the introductions for your site, please."

► Let people know if you are audio- or videotaping the meeting, and what the procedure will be to get copies of the tape.

FIRST THINGS FIRST (continued)

Ground Rules

► Spend a few minutes reviewing videoconferencing guidelines. This can greatly affect how much you accomplish during the rest of your time "on the air." This is especially important in a multipoint meeting.

- Remind participants to pause after speaking to allow time for a response—because of the slight delay in audio transmission, a moment of silence does not necessarily mean no one else has anything to say. You may find it helpful to suggest that speakers say "I'm done," when they've finished, to avoid confusion.

- Ask participants to state their name and site when they speak, to avoid confusion: "This is Pat in Phoenix and I have a question."

The Open-Mic Disaster

The president of XYZ Widget Corporation called a videoconference with his senior staff to share his plans for a new corporate direction. One senior manager, who was alone at his site, left his microphone on and then fell asleep. Every time the slumbering manager snored, his mic picked up the sound and the camera cut away from the company president to a picture of him asleep in his chair. The snores repeatedly interrupted the meeting until the fed-up company president shouted, "Wake up!" at him long-distance.

REMIND PEOPLE TO KEEP THEIR MICROPHONES
MUTED UNTIL THEY WISH TO SPEAK.

THREE KEY SKILLS FOR VIDEOCONFERENCE MEETINGS

SKILL #1: Using the Camera Effectively

Close-ups versus Group Shots

► Be aware of the subliminal effect of apparent image size on receiving monitors.

- In wide-angle shots, several people can be on screen at once, but they will appear smaller. This can create a subtle feeling of distance.

- In a close-up, the person's head will be closer to life-size, and it will seem more as if the person is in the same room.

► Remember that in a group shot, facial expressions and reactions will be harder to read at the remote sites. Switch to a close-up periodically to minimize the distancing effect of group shots.

► Use a close-up shot when someone is asking or answering a question.

► Use a close-up shot of yourself for maximum impact when you need to reestablish control of the meeting.

► Use a wide shot of your site as a "generic" outgoing image whenever no one at your location is speaking.

Voice-Activated versus Director Control

► Use voice-activated mode when you want to get a discussion going.

► Use director control mode when you want to turn to a new topic, get the discussion back on track or mediate a disagreement.

► Switch to director control in a lively discussion to avoid problems when the camera has trouble keeping up with shifting voice locations.

► In voice-activated mode, say something before sending a graphic, so the camera will switch to you—otherwise the graphic may seem out of context to viewers.

► Use director control while you are playing a videotape, so the picture doesn't switch to a remote site if someone coughs.

THREE KEY SKILLS FOR VIDEOCONFERENCE MEETINGS (continued)

SKILL #2: Leading Discussions

Use Questions Effectively

► Use questions to:

- Probe for additional information: "What else can you tell us about that market?"

- Shift a discussion to other areas: "How has the data from the focus groups been incorporated into our marketing plan?"

- Refocus the discussion: "Can you summarize the three most important points from your report?"

- Clarify unclear statements: "Could you give us an example of that, please?"

► When a question is asked, call on someone at another site to answer rather than responding yourself. Check back with the questioner to make sure the question has been answered satisfactorily.

Keep Things Moving

► Suggest how to make the meeting more effective: "I think we're going in circles here. Why doesn't each site take a few minutes to decide on their top priorities, then we'll try to reach an agreement."

► Take a break if discussion bogs down. Give everyone five minutes to get up and move around, get coffee, etc.

Stay on Schedule

► State your meeting objective as the first order of business. Refer back to this objective to keep discussions on track.

► Keep an "Issues Board" (on a white board or piece of paper) of items that come up in discussion that are not directly relevant or that you plan to address later in the meeting. This will help you keep to your agenda and schedule.

► Take a few minutes at the end of the meeting to review the Issues Board. If you have the option of extending the meeting, lead a group decision whether to table or discuss issues that remain unaddressed.

SKILL #3: Managing Participation

▶ Use column six of your storyboard to track participation.

- Place an X next to a person's name each time he or she is heard from.

- Place a question mark next to a person's name each time he or she asks a question.

NEW YORK	Ken Miller	XX?X
	Jim Smith	XX
	Karen Gregory	?
	Susan Warren	XXX
LOS ANGELES	Bill Gold	
	Maria Gutierrez	X?
	Pat Wilson	????
SINGAPORE	Caroline Wang	?XX
	Tony DeNobile	X?X?XXX
	Steve Strauss	X

In this example, Tony DeNobile is dominating the discussions, Bill Gold hasn't spoken up yet, and Pat Wilson has lots of questions:

- Keep the discussion on track: "Pat, you have a lot of questions about the small widget configuration. If we all need clarification, I can get Jill Smalley to join us by telephone, or we can move on to our next agenda item and Pat can call Jill after the meeting. What would the New York group like to do? Singapore, would you like to stick with the design issue or move on?" etc.

- Call on the quiet ones: "Bill in L.A., we haven't heard your opinion on this yet."

- If you ask, "Does anyone else have any comments?" either several people will answer at once, or no one will respond. Instead, call on a site you haven't heard much from: "Who in Los Angeles would like to add to that?"

IMPORTANT THINGS TO REMEMBER

1. Videoconferencing systems have a limited capacity to digest and display motion.

If you are a fidgeter, you may have to learn to restrain your movements during a videoconference.

- Avoid unconscious mannerisms such as rubbing your nose or brushing hair from your face; they are distracting in a video image, especially in close-up.

- Put down your pen or pencil when you are not writing so you won't unconsciously waggle it or tap it on the table.

- Do not rock or tip your chair.

- Maintain a consistent distance from the camera; when you lean forward or backward your movement will appear exaggerated.

- Assume that you are always on camera, even when you are not speaking.

I need to remember not to: _____

_____

_____

2. Eye contact with remote sites requires looking at the camera, not at the other people in your room.

People at other sites will feel like observers, not participants, unless you consciously look at the camera as much as possible.

- Since the main camera is usually positioned above the monitor, it may be easier to remember to look at the monitor, not the camera.

- Think in terms of looking through the camera to remote sites. Pretend that you are talking to a good friend sitting across the room from you.

I will remind myself to make eye contact by: _____

_____

_____

3. In a multipoint meeting, you can't see everyone at all sites at all times.

You can see only one remote site at a time, and the image you receive from that site may be a close-up shot of one person, leaving others off-screen.

- Switch to group shots periodically to help everyone stay "in touch."

- The more locations involved in your meeting, the easier it is to leave one or more sites out of the discussion for extended periods of time. Make sure you involve or check in on all sites regularly throughout the meeting.

I plan to maintain contact with remote sites by: _____

_____

_____

4. It may be difficult to keep people's attention, especially in a multipoint meeting.

Participants who are not speaking will have little to do but watch a monitor, and it will be easy for them to slip into a passive mode or become inattentive.

- Be careful not to slouch. Your relaxed posture will send a message that you are not fully involved, and will imply that participants don't need to be attentive, either.

- Review your storyboard to make sure you have planned a variety of pacing and visual stimuli.

- Have some prepared questions or small group discussion activities on hand to use if you sense participation lagging.

I plan to keep people's attention by: _____

_____

_____

WHAT TO DO IF YOU HAVE TECHNICAL TROUBLE

Video

1. If you have trouble with the video connection, explain that you are having difficulties and continue with the meeting, if you can, over the audio channel.

2. You may be able to transmit graphics over a fax line if the video connection can't be fixed.

Audio

1. Use the document camera and a hand-written notice to explain that you have lost audio.

2. If a technician is available to try to fix the problem, use the document camera to ask participants to stand by.

3. If you ask remote sites to stand by, don't leave them hanging for more than a few minutes without an update.

4. Give people something to do while they wait, such as discussing the next agenda item among themselves while audio is down.

When a Problem Can't Be Fixed

1. If a remote site has a persistent problem, don't waste everyone else's time trying to fix it. Ask the site with the problem to shut down and offer to tape the rest of the meeting for them.

2. If problems persist among multiple sites or if audio problems can't be fixed, discontinue the meeting. You may wish to reconvene as a telephone conference.

ENDING THE VIDEOCONFERENCE

Saying Goodbye

At the end of the meeting, thank everyone for their participation and take a moment to remind people of any follow-up actions they are to take.

If minutes have been prepared during the meeting, ask participants to remain at their sites for a few minutes while the minutes are faxed to them. Otherwise, let participants know when and how minutes will be circulated.

Getting Feedback

For your first few videoconferences, ask for feedback from those attending. Provide participants with a copy of the evaluation form on the following page. If possible, ask people to fax their comments back to you before they leave the meeting site. You may also choose to telephone a few participants after the videoconference and ask them for feedback.

Evaluating Yourself

Take a few moments immediately following the meeting to evaluate how things went. What worked well? What didn't? What would you like to handle differently next time?

The sooner you do this the better. If you leave it until the end of the day, or until the next morning, you risk losing useful ideas. Take a photocopy of the form (which may be reproduced without further permission from the publisher) on the next page to the meeting, and fill it out on the spot. Then review it while you are planning your next videoconference meeting.

Videoconference Evaluation

Date:	Meeting:
What do you feel was most successful about this videoconference?	
What was least successful?	
What would you like to do differently next time?	
Other comments	

THANK YOU FOR YOUR PARTICIPATION!

Please fax this page to: _____ at: ( ) _____

FOLLOW-UP MEMO

During the videoconference, you and your colleagues are likely to have made some decisions about the future. Since the videoconference that brought you all together is now over, it's a good idea to summarize and remind people of next steps. If your system includes a networked computer, you can use it to record decisions, results of brainstorming sessions, etc. These can be easily formatted and displayed for a summary review at the end of the meeting, then faxed to remote sites for participants to take away with them. Use this page to plan a follow-up memo that will provide at-a-glance information about:

► Decisions made _____

_____

► Issues that were tabled, and when they will be reexamined _____

_____

► Actions to be taken, and by whom _____

_____

► Any planned follow-up meetings/videoconferences _____

_____

► Names and contact numbers for participants or site leaders _____

_____

► Where and how to get a copy of any audio- or videotapes made of the meeting _____

_____

SECRET TO SUCCESS

The best way to learn how to lead an effective videoconference is to do it!

SECTION VII

Appendixes

APPENDIX A: TOOLS

Videoconference Planning Checklist

Use this checklist to track your planning and preparation activities.

☐ Define meeting purpose and objectives

☐ Include a number of sites and people per site that are appropriate to the purpose and objectives of your meeting

☐ Schedule videoconferencing rooms and/or equipment for all sites

☐ Arrange for technical assistance when/where needed

☐ Confirm attendance of all meeting participants

☐ Develop storyboard

☐ Send out premeeting participant letter and videoconferencing guidelines

☐ Prepare any handouts to be used during the meeting and circulate to all participants

☐ Create visuals/graphics

☐ Test visuals/graphics on the system to make sure they fit the aspect ratio and that resolution is adequate for video monitor display

☐ Test prerecorded videotapes on the system

☐ Check that all required peripherals (scanners, fax, VCR, etc.) are available and have been tested at all sites

☐ Test audio-only links if additional participants will be phoning in

☐ Practice your storyboard on the equipment, if possible

☐ Define seating arrangements for each site

☐ Establish camera presets for each site

☐ Adjust conference room lighting, if necessary

☐ Choose an appropriate outfit and accessories

Cost Comparison Worksheet

IN-PERSON MEETING		
Salaries	Meeting time and travel time for all participants	$
Benefits, taxes	35%–50% of salary. Check with personnel department	$
Travel costs	Mileage	$
	Tolls	$
	Parking	$
	Airfare	$
	Rental cars/Taxi	$
	Food	$
	Lodging	$
Room Charge	Cost of hotel meeting room (if applicable)	$
TOTAL		$

VIDEOCONFERENCE MEETING		
Salaries	Meeting time for all participants, plus travel time to videoconferencing sites, if other than the office	$
Benefits, taxes	Use same percentage as for in-person meeting	$
Travel costs (to videoconferencing sites, if other than office)	Mileage	$
	Tolls	$
	Parking	$
	Airfare	$
	Rental cars/Taxi	$
	Food	$
	Lodging	$
Network access	Cost to hook up to your carrier	$
Network usage	Long distance phone charges	$
	Usage fee for public switched network	$
Room charge	Total cost per hour for any public rooms, times length of meeting	$
TOTAL COST		$

Videoconference Storyboard

STORYBOARD FOR: _____

TIME	TOPIC	CONTENT/METHOD

Page: _____ of _____

SUPPORT	SYSTEM CUES	PARTICIPATION

APPENDIX B: GLOSSARY

ACCESS CHANNEL: Digital telecommunications line that connects you to your carrier.

ASPECT RATIO: The relationship between the width and height of a television or video display monitor. NTSC (American format) and PAL (European format) televisions and monitors have an aspect ratio of 4:3.

BANDWIDTH: The amount of data that can be transmitted by your channel, measured in bits per second (bps) and referred to as a bit rate. The higher the bandwidth, the more information can be transmitted.

BANDWIDTH ON DEMAND: The ability to use multiple channels to provide greater bandwidth. Both transmitting and receiving sites must have an inverse multiplexer (I-Mux) to take advantage of multiple 56K or 64K channels.

BRIDGE: The device that enables three or more videoconferencing sites to communicate. Also called a multipoint control unit (MCU).

BUFFER: A memory device for temporary storage of digital information, such as a graphic or video image, during or before transmission.

CARRIER: A provider of local and/or long-distance phone services. AT&T, MCI and U.S. Sprint are carriers that offer videoconferencing services to their customers.

CODEC: Short for coder/decoder, the codec is the heart of the videoconferencing system. The send-site codec turns analog information into digital data and compresses it for transmission. The receive-site codec decompresses and decodes the data back into audio and video signals.

CODEC CONVERSION: Codecs from different manufacturers may not be able to understand each other. Codec conversion adds a translation step to the process. Conversion service is offered by carriers such as AT&T, MCI and U.S. Sprint.

COMPRESSION: Compression is essential to videoconferencing, since it reduces the amount of data to be transmitted between sites. Video signals are compressed by reducing the number of frames per second or by transmitting only data that has changed from the previous frame.

DEDICATED ACCESS: A private, leased telephone line connecting your site to your long-distance service provider.

DELAY: The time required for the audio signal to pass between a sender and a receiver and through each of their codecs. Although this delay is short, it is noticeable.

DESKTOP VIDEOCONFERENCING: Use of a personal computer for videoconferencing.

DIAL-UP: The ability to arrange a multipoint videoconference by "dialing up" remote site telephone numbers. Requires connection to a switched access network.

DOCUMENT CAMERA: A camera specifically designed to take pictures of paper-based information (such as photographs, diagrams, or text) or small objects during a videoconference.

DUAL 56: Two 56K digital phone lines combined to create a 112K channel for low-bandwidth videoconferencing.

FRAME: A single visual image. Videoconferencing systems transmit between 8 and 30 frames per second (fps), depending on the bandwidth used.

FRAME DROPPING: In low bandwidth (i.e., slow transmission) systems, the technique of skipping or dropping video frames to stay in real time.

FRAME GRAB: The ability to capture and store a video frame so that it can be saved, printed or manipulated as a graphic.

INVERSE MULTIPLEXER (I-Mux): The device that enables a videoconferencing system to use multiple digital channels for greater bandwidth. Both send and receive sites must have an I-Mux to take advantage of this capability.

ISDN: Integrated Services Digital Network—a standard for digital communication.

ITCA: International Teleconferencing Association—a professional association that promotes audio- and videoteleconferencing.

LAN: Local Area Network—the interconnection of a group of computers and peripheral devices (such as printers and servers), usually within one office or department of an organization.

APPENDIX B: GLOSSARY (continued)

LEASED LINE: Dedicated lines leased from a carrier by an organization for its exclusive use for point-to-point videoconferencing.

MCU: Multipoint control unit—the device that connects three or more sites for a multipoint videoconference, and that switches audio and video signals between sites.

NETWORK: Multiple computers (or other devices) connected together so that data can be transmitted between and among them.

PERIPHERALS: Add-ons to a videoconferencing system that broaden its capabilities. Common peripherals include document cameras, scanners, VCRs and personal computers.

PICTURE-IN-PICTURE: The ability to display two video pictures simultaneously on one monitor. In a single-monitor videoconferencing system, this allows the outgoing image to be displayed in a small window in the corner of the incoming image.

PRIVATE NETWORK: A network of leased lines providing point-to-point links between multiple locations within one organization.

PROPRIETARY ALGORITHM: The specific code that a codec uses to compress and decompress digital images. Different codec manufacturers use different proprietary algorithms, which can lead to compatibility problems between different systems. See codec conversion.

PUBLIC ROOM: A videoconferencing center that rents use of its videoconferencing systems at an hourly rate to the public. Public rooms provide complete technical support services to their customers.

RESOLUTION: The degree of detail provided by a video system. Lower bandwidths result in lower resolution.

ROLL-ABOUT: A compact videoconferencing system, in which the codec, camera(s), monitor(s), audio system, etc., are designed as a self-contained unit, usually on a wheeled cart.

SCANNER: A device that takes an optical image of a photograph, diagram or text on paper and translates it into digital information.

SWITCHED 56: A kind of service, independent of any specific carrier, that allows customers to dial up and transmit digital information (up to 56K per second per channel) as if they were making a regular long-distance telephone call.

VIDEO SCAN CONVERTER: A device that enables the images generated by a personal computer to be displayed on a videoconferencing monitor.

VOICE-ACTIVATED: The videoconferencing mode in which the audio pickup is routed to whomever speaks loudest. Cameras can be linked to the voice-activated microphones, so that both audio and video are automatically switched to the person speaking.

NOTES

OVER 150 BOOKS AND 35 VIDEOS AVAILABLE IN THE 50-MINUTE SERIES

We hope you enjoyed this book. If so, we have good news for you. This title is part of the best-selling *50-MINUTE*™ *Series* of books. All *Series* books are similar in size and identical in price. Many are supported with training videos.

To order *50-MINUTE* Books and Videos or request a free catalog, contact your local distributor or Crisp Publications, Inc., 1200 Hamilton Court, Menlo Park, CA 94025. Our toll-free number is (800) 442-7477.

50-Minute Series Books and Videos Subject Areas . . .

Management
Training
Human Resources
Customer Service and Sales Training
Communications
Small Business and Financial Planning
Creativity
Personal Development
Wellness
Adult Literacy and Learning
Career, Retirement and Life Planning

Other titles available from Crisp Publications in these categories

Crisp Computer Series
The Crisp Small Business & Entrepreneurship Series
Quick Read Series
Management
Personal Development
Retirement Planning